# SELLING YOUR HOUSE TO

# A CASH INVESTOR

## REAL STORIES OF SAFE, FAST, AS-IS HOME SALES

### SAUL  Z

ISBN: 978-1-08-244463-0

# TABLE OF CONTENTS

# WHO IS THIS BOOK FOR? AND WHO IS THIS BOOK NOT FOR?

I wanted to write a book for sellers who want to sell property to a cash investor, and who probably have a lot of questions about the process. They want to know things like, "How legit is this?" and, "Where is the catch?"

They want to know whether they can sell their home safely and without losing money. They want to know whether the transaction can be done quickly, and whether they're committing to anything just by asking for an offer.

It's important to define who this book is not for, though. This book is not for a homeowner who has a home in tip-top shape who just wants to save on real estate commission by selling to an investor.

This book is not for someone who doesn't have a need to sell in the next few months, or who is looking to get more than the retail value.

This book is not for someone who has a problem knowing that investors will have to make an offer that allows fair profit for renovating the home and reselling or renting it.

This book is not for someone who has the time and money to fix the property themselves, who is comfortable with showings by and to strangers, or who is comfortable paying commissions and closing costs.

If you have no problem dealing with appraisers, banks, real estate agents, inspectors, village codes and requirements, and attorneys, and you have no immediate need to move, this book is not for you.

This book is for sellers who want to sell their as-is home for cash directly to investors without the hassles and fees that come with selling on the retail market. It's for people who want to sell it at a fair price at which an investor can fix the property and make their own profit afterward.

Most people don't know this, but there are a significant number of homes in the United States that are sold without an agent (the National Association of Realtors puts that number at about 13%). That means about 1 in 10 sellers are choosing to skip the traditional process and sell directly to an investor or another homeowner.

It's perfectly legit and it happens quite often. Although it's absolutely safe to sell to a cash investor, it's critical that the seller is cautious, informed, and makes sure they are working with a reputable company. This book is a collection of testimonials that cover a variety of circumstances, each of which reveals an important part of the process for every seller.

It wasn't always easy to research home buyers, but now there are a host of powerful tools at the seller's disposal. They can check out investors through the Better Business Bureau (BBB) and read reviews on internet sites like Google or Facebook that detail the experiences of other sellers.

Sellers will typically receive less money than they would get by using an agent through the retail market, but at the same time, there are a tremendous number of benefits:

- You won't need to fix the property
- You won't pay commissions or closing costs

- You won't have to clean the property or handle inspector-requested repairs
- You can avoid dealing with lenders and banks
- You can pick the closing date of your choosing
- … and you can sometimes even get a cash advance prior to closing.

When you put the benefits into perspective and your situation fits, selling to a cash investor can be a gain rather than a loss -- and it's not uncommon that an investor can actually save a house from various default sales or auctions so that the seller doesn't lose their entire equity in the home.

In terms of timeline, selling to an investor can happen as quickly as 7 days depending on title clearance. In my company, we encountered a seller who had an extremely urgent situation that we were able to close in just 48 hours (most of our sellers choose to close in about 30 days).

Typically, a seller -- not the investor -- chooses the date on which they want to close, which is the opposite of selling to a retail buyer that requests a specific closing date. And with a cash investor, a seller doesn't commit to anything by requesting an offer. There is no obligation to accept it or reject it. An answer of "No" is perfectly acceptable. Our company doesn't expect to buy every home, and every seller should not expect to sell to every investor. As long as we can give our best shot to working out a mutually beneficial offer, we're good with that.

# WHY DID I DECIDE TO WRITE THIS BOOK?

After being in real estate for over a decade, I realize that there are quite a few people who don't want to deal with the traditional way of selling a home. And it took me years to realize that by working as a licensed real estate broker, you are conditioned by the industry to get the highest price. That sounds good, but in the end, it isn't always right for the seller.

Ironically, it's true only from a real estate agent's perspective. The higher the price, the more commission agents make – and that doesn't work for those 1 in 10 who can't or don't want to go through the expensive, time-consuming home repair process that can maximize the value. It doesn't work for the people who simply don't want to deal with all the things that come along with selling. It doesn't work for the people who put more value on a quick, no-hassle sale than on making sure they sell for the absolute highest dollar amount (when and if that sale actually happens).

After buying homes directly from sellers, I had another realization: they are underserved in the market because many of them have some type of situation that can't be addressed by a traditional real estate agent. These situations can fall in three categories: a Money Problem, a Property Problem, or a No Hassle Problem.

A 'money problem' seller could be some type of default on taxes, a mortgage, a bankruptcy, etc. in which the seller needs to sell the home quickly. There's just not enough time to put it on the market, or it's too risky for them to deal with a retail buyer.

A 'property problem' seller could have an outdated home, damage to the property, code violations, hazardous conditions, or any issue that makes the home a poor fit for a retail buyer.

The 'no hassle' seller tends to be someone who may have inherited a home from a relative or simply wants to move on as smoothly and easily as possible. Sometimes they're not as personally invested in the property; other times their lives are so busy that they just can't handle the traditional realty process, especially if they're living in a different city or state.

No matter which of those three scenarios describes your situation, cash investors can solve the problem. What I've learned over more transactions than I can count is that our sellers are much more grateful and appreciative for solving their problem compared to the ones I represented as a real estate broker and selling retail.

Retail sellers, for the most part, are not the happiest campers. I don't blame them. Deciding to sell a home retail is a lot to take on, and most of the time they blame the agent, the market, the buyer, the attorney, the title company, or anyone else in the long, complicated process -- and the more that process drags on, the more likely it is that something can go wrong.

With all that in mind, I decided to write a book about what it's really like selling to a cash investor. I've interviewed a range of our clients who all shared their experience selling directly to an investor. Each story summarizes their situation and reveals how they felt about the process. They show what made them comfortable and why they chose -- or didn't choose – a potential investor. After each story, I offer an important lesson that will help you understand how to feel confident about working with a cash investor and, ultimately, to determine whether that process is the right fit for you.

# 1

## DIANE: A TRADITIONAL CASH INVESTOR SALE

D iane found herself in a very common scenario: she'd inherited her parents' cozy three-bedroom, two-bathroom house, but plans to keep it in the family just didn't materialize. At a certain point she started thinking about whether it would be worth it to go through the process of renovations, working with a realtor, dealing with showings, and worrying about how it would all turn out.

**IN HER WORDS:** "It was my family's house, where I grew up. When my mom and dad passed away, they left the house to my kids. I was the liaison between everything, I was taking care of everything including power of attorney, and we wanted to make a decision together about what to do.

"We were in the next town over. My brother and sister-in-law were living in the house for a while. Then we thought that when my daughter graduated from college, she would move into the house with her friends… but then that all fell through.

"Everyone else had other plans, and my son wasn't ready to move into a house on his own. We just thought the best thing to do would be to sell it, but we didn't really know how to go about it. Then we got a card about selling the house as-is and I thought that might be perfect.

"My dad was pretty handy; he was a carpenter. He did a lot of work on the house, but as he was ailing it was harder for him to do things that needed updating, like painting, new furnishing, and the kitchen floor. The house really needed some updating and the kitchen was a total mess. It needed so much work that we wanted the burden taken off us. By working with an investor, we wouldn't have to worry about figuring out how to fix it up and sell it.

"My parents bought the house in 1952 and the previous owners had tile all over the kitchen. The floor had regular linoleum, but the walls and ceiling were yellow with a dark green and a mint green. It was very outdated and we thought, "Nobody would want this!" It was a big job to even think about what to do.

"The house was livable and we had so many good memories. I brought my kids home there when they were born, for holidays… we spent a lot of time there. Since we lived just 5 minutes away, I was always over there with my family.

"At first, we thought we could call a few different realtors we knew, or go through the hassle of selling by owner as a fixer upper. I didn't like the idea of wondering who would be coming over to see the house, or anyone walking around in my parents' house… it just bothered me. By going through a realtor, they'd take over the process and have people walking through the house, too – and then get a cut from selling it.

"We called an investor to give them a chance because we wanted to see what they'd say. It was a good starting point and we wanted to see what they had to offer. When the agent came over, we felt so comfortable. I liked everything she talked about and I didn't feel like there was any pressure. That took a lot of the burden off us.

"It was hard enough going through my parents' house and packing things up. There was stuff there from when my grandparents had the house, and that was a hard thing to do. The agent took a lot of pressure off me.

"She explained the process and how we wouldn't have to fix anything up. She even said that we could leave anything we didn't want to pack up and move and they would take care of it. We left a few things there so we didn't have to worry about cleaning up or dumping everything out.

"We did some cleaning and had a few garage sales, but that's really all I had to do. I told my family, "Look around, see what you want. And anything else we'll either try to sell or just leave here." It was a lot less pressure and a lot less hassle.

"There are just so many house-flipping shows where people aren't sure what they're doing. I really liked the idea that this renovation would be done by professionals. They were going to make the house beautiful and everything would be done right and done safely. Then I knew it would be an enjoyable home for a new family.

"The contractor was always in touch with us, too. If he needed to get people to do some painting or take up the carpeting, he'd call and ask if we were available. We even talked back and forth with the agent because she seemed like an old friend. Sometimes we would just sit and chat.

"As we got further into the process, the lawyer was helpful as well. He would send us email lists and papers if we needed to sign them... he was always on top of everything. I was asking him questions about whether I had to call the Village Hall, and he said, "Don't worry about anything, I'm taking care of it for you." He made me feel at ease that I wouldn't do something wrong or forget anything. I knew everything was being done correctly.

"This process was a godsend for me. It was simple – one phone call and it fell into place. My dad has been gone five years now, and I still hear his voice telling me, "Everything will fall into place, it always does." That held true through the whole process of selling the house.

"Eventually my husband and I want to retire. We're thinking about Texas, and he said, "Well, you know, when we're ready to leave we could just call them again to sell our house." That's down the road a little bit, but we really enjoyed the process and not having to worry about anything."

**HER LESSON:** Diane's scenario was fairly traditional with an inherited house that needed some work before it was ready to sell. There weren't any unique aspects to her problem the way there were in Denise's situation; she and her family just faced dealing with a major project that was potentially overwhelming. The payoff of that stress wasn't there, and the most important thing for Diane was to make sure that a new family would get a home that meant as much to them as it did to her, and to get to that point with as little stress as possible. By finding an investor and team that she trusted, Diane was able to feel good about wrapping up the home sale and knowing that every element of the process was done right. As she said, "No worries. No hassles. It's all taken care of."

# 2

## CINDY: DO YOUR HOMEWORK ON OFFERS

Cindy had a large five-bedroom, two-full and one-half bath home in an area that included extremely high property taxes. Over time her home needed some repairs, so she decided that she had to move to a more affordable area.

But Cindy didn't want to work with a traditional realtor because she had a very unique environment: as a breeder of exotic pets, she wasn't sure that her home would be attractive to the average buyer despite its spacious, airy rooms. She recognized that a realtor might force her to re-style the home so the market would receive it better, which would be a serious disruption to her business and an inconvenience.

She decided that her best option was to work with a cash investor. When she met with the first investor, she was anything but happy with both the low offer and the manner in which it was presented to her. Eventually she found a cash investor that could work with her situation, communicate very clearly, and offer her a good price.

**IN HER WORDS:** "Financially, I couldn't afford to keep up my house. The property taxes were outrageous. The house just went downhill, and I had to get rid of it to move to where I'm at right now, which is much easier. I'm very appreciative of it.

"Honestly, I didn't have the time to clean up the house because it was very large. And I have lots of exotic pets, so it just wouldn't look good for me to sell it the way it was. I have a business breeding and selling exotic animals like bearded dragons, veiled chameleons and coatimundis, a cousin of the raccoon. Plus, I breed insects like crickets, so it's a freak-out in most people's eyes. The only people who would think that was cool were the ones who were in a trade like mine.

"I just knew what I had to do, and it was time for me to move on. I had to go because the house was huge. It was just me and my son, my boyfriend at the time -- he's now my husband -- and my brother.

"When I decided to sell, I had someone come out to the house. And I was very unhappy with his bid.

"Their offer was ridiculously low, and I could just tell the guy was not interested in buying anything like my house. I don't know... I know they were home buyers, but he went through the house very quickly and I could tell he was disinterested. He made an offer that was so low that I knew it was worth more than that. Between his attitude and his offer, there was no way I was going to sell to him.

"And then another agency came in. I was totally impressed. I met the agent and she was awesome. The offer was decent and she was very thorough about everything down to a T. She explained each step of what was going to happen, how long it would take, and mapped out the process. Then she led me through it, and she knew what she was talking about, that's for sure.

"I knew the offer was enough money for me to afford a new home and have a little bit extra, so I just said, "Yep, we're doing it."

"After closing the deal, I had two more days to move out. You think you have it all, but you don't, and it's easy to put it off until the last minute. We'd been moving for weeks before because I had already purchased the other home and because I have reptiles, I couldn't be in two places at once. I don't ever want to move again!

"But I totally recommend selling to a cash investor. They were so upfront, and they answered questions that I'm sure I asked more than once. Everything went so smoothly that if I made a phone call to the agent, she would be right there on it.

"I'm happy they were the second ones that came into my situation. I felt that they were honest people. It's a scary world out there, and you never know what's going to happen or what kind of BS someone is going to pull off. Not everyone is a good person, but they were.

"I'm happy that I moved out, I'm comfortable in my new home, and I'm not pressured by the bills I was getting killed with out there. If I had just accepted the first offer that came through, it wouldn't have worked out nearly as well for me."

**HER LESSON:** Cindy's circumstances were unique, and she realized immediately that cash investors can be great partners for non-traditional sales. But she also realized that not every cash investor is trying to strike a deal that works for both parties.

Cindy did her homework and recognized that her first offer was not necessarily going to be her best offer. Then she found a cash investor who valued her home and led her through the process. By making sure she worked with the right partner, she was able to sell her house comfortably and move to a new house that was a much better fit for her, her family, and her business.

SAUL Z

# 3

## DAN: RESEARCH UNTIL YOU FEEL COMFORTABLE

D an and his brother were charged with selling the family home after his father's passing. Dan is a commercial real estate project manager, so he was perfectly capable of handling a renovation and sale on the four-bedroom, two-full bathroom home. After researching the process and realizing that the best solution for their family was a quick sale – especially once his mother's health required that she be closer to her sons – Dan took the next step with a cash investor.

**IN HIS WORDS:** "I was dealing with selling my mother's house, and she was the one living in it. I'm married with children and living in a different suburb, but I was the primary point of contact for the transaction.

"It was the house that I grew up in from when I was five years old. My mother lived in the house for over 40 years. It was a family home for me and my parents and my brother, and we lived there for a long time. My father recently passed, and he was in that house with her, too.

"From a financial standpoint it was my mother's house, so we had nothing to do with that aspect. From a family perspective, my brother and I were helping my mother make the transaction happen so she could transition to new accommodations.

"She was living in the house alone ever since my dad passed, and she's in relatively good health. But her knee is not so great and there are stairs in the house... not a lot of stairs, but there are stairs. We really wanted to move her to a place that didn't have stairs and also move her closer to us. My brother and I live ten minutes apart and her house was about a half-hour drive from us.

"We wanted to move her closer to us and closer to her church, but she just did not want to leave the house. She said, "I don't want to leave the house, I'm going to die in this house." That was her perspective... until her knee started giving her problems. Then it was time to go.

"I talked to her about relocating. Eventually, we started to explore. I kind of wore her out, and she saw the flyer from Saul. We actually have multiple friends who are real estate agents and one is a close family member. One is an in-law, and I was keeping him apprised step-by-step on this whole process. He was all for selling to an investor. He wanted what's best for our family and he wanted what's best for my mom.

"He agreed that selling to an investor was a good deal from a risk standpoint, from a timing standpoint, from a surety standpoint. Could we have gotten a contractor and renovated the house and made a lot of money? Potentially, but there's risk in that, and my mother's tolerance for risk is not what an investor's tolerance for risk is when they do this every day for a living.

"Could we have sold the house as-is to the general public and let somebody else renovate it? Yeah, we could have done that, too, and listed it with our family member. But selling to an investor seemed to be the best approach for my mom to get things certain sooner.

"It was a good fit on many fronts given her circumstances. A risk averse option was a good option. If she was potentially more willing to take on risks, then maybe we'd have gone in a different direction.

"For most people renovating would be a big project, but I'm a project manager in a commercial real estate company. I do that every day for a living, so it wouldn't be a big deal for me. I work with contractors and subcontractors, architects, and engineers every single day, so I have the skills to do it.

"I did my analysis because I have a decent understanding of the market and the real estate agent that's in our family helped me understand it, too. We were able to see this was a good deal and that it made sense. Once I understood where we needed to be financially, with putting zero money into the house, we could sell it as-is doing nothing compared to what we would need to have done to make the house sellable on the market.

"My advice is to do your homework and get comfortable. Once you feel comfortable, you can pursue selling to an investor. You can't go in blind -- you've got be educated. There's so much information out there now between all the different websites on the internet that have to do with this kind of stuff, but once you feel comfortable and educated, then you can take a step that you feel confident in.

"Like our sale, after we called the first time, they sent out two associates to look at the house to see if they were interested. Honestly, one of them just sat with my mother because she was still kind of on the fence of 'Do I sell, do I not sell.' She just sat with my mother and talked. They connected, which made her more comfortable and that helped to move her. I think she was already pretty much there, but it didn't hurt to feel more comfortable. If anything, it helped the process a little bit more.

"I think that process is good for the seller's side, too, because if you make a connection with people, they're less likely to back out of deals as opposed to when it's all about money. To me, real estate is the relationship game. You need to make relationships, even if they're short-term relationships. You still need to foster those.

"When the investor came in and closed the deal, he was a tough negotiator, but he was fair."

**HIS LESSON:** In real estate – as in most parts of our life – relationships mean everything. Dan's points about doing enough research to feel educated about the process are extremely important, but even the most knowledgeable person won't be happy with the transaction unless they feel comfortable along the way. Talk to your investor and make sure that you can ask them any question you want. Make sure they feel comfortable talking to you, too. If it doesn't feel right, it probably isn't.

Even though you're trying to sell a home quickly and with minimal extra work, the comfort and peace of mind that comes with finding the right fit is invaluable in the long-term.

# 4

## GARY: BEWARE OF RENOVATIONS... AND DISTANCE

G ary and his brothers were tasked with fixing up their parents' house. They started the renovation process on the three-bedroom, one-full and one-half bathroom home. Gary soon found that it was incredibly difficult and stressful to manage it all while living in another time zone. After a few misses with electricians as winter approached, they recognized that they weren't sure that their stress and investment would even pay off.

**IN HIS WORDS:** "We were selling because my mother had passed away. The house was in Chicago and we were doing our best to clear it out and fix it up. But I'm in Virginia, so I was 700 miles away as the trustee for the house. We tried to line up contracts, but it got to the point where delays kept things from happening. That's when we started to think it might be better to sell the house as-is rather than try to fix it up on our own.

"It was just hard to manage from a distance. Part of the problem was the local inspection. The town required an inspection and we knew that the electrical system needed to be upgraded. The house was built in 1949. My parents were the original owners, so nothing had been updated for decades. It probably would have needed a lot of things updated and corrected including the electrical.

"I had two brothers who were checking on the house. We were trying to get things done, but everyone was working. It was just tough to try to make the time to devote to the house and to take care of our own stuff. I was out there a few times trying to help things along… we did our best, but we couldn't really get the time to be there to fix it up.

"For months we tried to get quotes from electricians. We didn't like a couple of the quotes we got, and then there was a long delay in getting a third quote. One of my brothers was approached by an investor for an as-is sale – I called, spoke with one of the employees, and then she did a site visit with one of my brothers. We wanted a fast resolution, and it looked like they would be able to do it quickly and would take over the problem of fixing up the house.

"We liked that they had a website; they seemed like a much more professional organization [than others]. We got another quote from a guy with a truck who just showed up… he wasn't with a real company. I liked it to be more professional.

"It was a little stressful for us to have just a one-day turnaround for the quote, but that's just the force of this. They said they were going to give us a quote and we'd have 24 hours to agree to it or not. That was a little pressure, but I accepted that and understood it.

"On the whole, there wasn't any problem. The overall process was stressful to me simply because I was 700 miles away and I'm doing everything on the phone… it had been several months, my mother had passed away, and we were still trying to do something with the house. So for me, all of that was stressful, but once the process started it was pretty smooth.

"The big advantage is that we could bring it to closure before the weather hit. Winter was coming and my brothers are all older and working full-time. It's just not easy to get to the house. In the winter, they'd be worrying about being responsible for the house in the freezing cold, and worrying about what could happen at the house that could cause damage. It was a relief to sell it.

"Our final water bill with the town included an updated plot survey, updated HVAC inspection, and one or two other things. I didn't know that was coming because our contract didn't specify those details, I just thought you pay the final water bill that you owe. But the attorney who represented me at the closing reached an agreement with the investment team, so I was very happy that they took care of those things.

"If I had been closer, I would've been able to talk to the town more and get more information about what's involved in the closing process and selling – just researching more about what the picture is. But I was very happy with the sale because it went smoothly and it happened within the 30 days that we were shooting for.

"Working with a well-established company sold me as much as the offer. Because again, another investor might not have been able to come up with the money, or they might have had other issues. It was easy to check them out.

"In any kind of home transaction, a sale is tough and there are no guarantees in any of it. So, you always wonder if you should have held out for more money, or what the market's going to do in four months. But I know that as the seller, I didn't want to have the house for another several months into the year while still trying to go through the process of fixing it up with no guarantees that we were going to make the money back on the sale. So, I was very happy to just go forward and sell it as-is."

**HIS LESSON:** Gary and his brothers experienced firsthand how difficult the renovation process can be. Those hurdles can include local laws, a gauntlet of contractors, and stress in the face of uncertainty. Throw in the complexity of trying to manage it all from a distance and the outlook can change fast.

Sometimes those outside factors like local regulations, logistics, or simply weather can make a traditional renovation process too hard and too expensive. It's important to take stock of all the factors that go into your decision to sell a property, and especially the ones that are out of your control. A professional, trustworthy investor can be an effective solution when the numbers – financial or blood pressure! -- just don't work with a realtor.

# 5

## DENISE: GOOD CASH INVESTORS CAN HANDLE ANYTHING

**D**enise and her sister were put in an almost unimaginable place: after their father passed, they found out that not only did his three-bedroom, one-bathroom house have severe problems, but there was also a second mortgage no one knew about. Between their grief, breaking the news to their grandmother, and wondering what to do with a property they loved, they faced a difficult decision about how to make the best of a tragic situation.

**IN HER WORDS:** "Okay well, I'm trying not to get sad because it's coming up on a year of my dad's passing...

"The house was my grandmother's, my dad lived there with her. Grandma went into a nursing home about six years ago and my dad was suffering from some sort of depression. We didn't know and he didn't, either.

"We'd see him all the time, but he was either at my sister's house or my house. Every time we'd try to go visit, he'd say, "Oh, I'll come by you guys," or if I would try to stop by he'd say he wasn't going to be home then. We thought that was strange, but we've all got our own lives and we'd see him all the time anyway. And then my Dad passed.

"We weren't notified. He didn't show up at my grandmother's nursing home, so my Grandmother sent the authorities over there. He had passed away in his rocking chair and was there for about probably eight days.

"So, the house was in pretty bad shape from his passing, as you can imagine, and then the house turned out to be a hoarding situation which we didn't know about. We just didn't realize what was going on.

"It was like you see on the hoarder TV shows. Things around the house were falling apart… this was my grandmother's home where I'd spent years as a kid, so it was very hard for us to cope with the situation. It was dirty and the water wasn't working. The bathroom wasn't working properly and there were animals in the attic because there was a hole in the roof.

"Then as were going through everything we found out that he had second mortgage that my grandmother knew nothing about… she thought the house only had one more payment. It added up to layered problems for us and it was a very difficult situation with an uninhabitable house.

"We wanted to do the right thing instead of letting the house just rot. We thought we must do the right thing. It was terrible because they worked so hard for that house, and my dad was always trying to come up with a plan to get back on his feet… but he never was able to and he ran out of time. It was a cute little house and it was a nice little corner lot.

"My sister and I both own our homes. She has her own business, so they're always making ends meet. We kept asking, "Are we doing the right thing?" by selling, but when it was all said and done, I think the agent said it took them almost $100k to renovate, and neither one of us had that. We just don't have that kind of time or money. It was heartbreaking not only with the loss of my dad, but then also dealing with the house and my grandmother.

"She always wanted to leave us something. She's in a nursing home because she's 102 years old, and I had to tell her about the situation with the house. It broke her heart, but we had to. The agent really was emotionally there with us... the situation was such a loss for us on so many levels, but it felt like she really cared and was upset about it, too.

"She was so passionate. We knew the agency was making money on the deal, but we could tell it affected her, especially when she met my grandmother to sign the papers. And that really helped, because I was angry. I was trying to grieve for my dad, and now I'm angry about the house... I'm mad at the whole situation, but she really helped us. It felt like she cared.

"My biggest concern with the sale was us not being financially responsible at any point for anything. We were scared because, like I said, we both own our own homes and my sister has a small business with her husband. I've got my day to day stuff to do, so we didn't need anything else on our plates. We were scared of getting involved with the sale because we weren't sure how we would be connected. It was scary, but the agent was amazing and helped us through that process.

"We wanted to maintain my dad's dignity so that he wasn't the crazy old man who had animals in the attic and a house that was falling apart. There was so much emotion behind it all, and it would have been nice to have a second home to rent out to a family or something, but we can't go back now.

"It feels good to talk about it, because there are days where we wonder if we did the right thing financially. But this wasn't just a case of throwing on some new carpet... we've got to keep our heads up and get through our days without our dad."

**HER LESSON:** Denise's story shows that cash investors can be a miracle solution for people in extremely difficult situations – and it doesn't get much harder than what her family went through. Dealing with a death is bad enough; being surprised with a second mortgage on an uninhabitable house made it all that much harder. At that point, the best course of action for their family was to find an understanding investor who could clean the property, rehabilitate it, and help them make the best of a near-impossible situation.

# 6

## CAROLYN: FIND INVESTORS WHO HAVE THE MONEY

Carolyn had a two bedroom, two-bathroom house with two more bedrooms below grade, and she needed to sell it fast. She could have gone through a traditional realtor, but she knew that the repairs necessary to put the house on the market would be expensive and take much more time than she had. For her, the best solution was to work with a cash investor who could buy the house as-is.

But when she approached a few investors, she found that some made the process easier than others. Even though she received a fair offer from one investor, she realized that it wasn't as simple as making the deal and moving on. He needed approval from his team to back up the offer he'd made her.

Her preferred investor had the money ready to go, and that made all the difference to Carolyn. She was able to sell her house quickly at a fair price, and she left the deal happy.

**IN HER WORDS:** "I wanted to sell my house, and I wanted to sell my house quickly. I'd lived there 20 years, but I would have had to update it to sell it. I didn't want to have to do repairs to fix it up, then put it on the market, and then wait for it to sell.

"I talked to three people about selling the house. They were all cash investors. One made an offer, but the amount was too low and the other couldn't match it. I ended up working with Chicagoland Home Buyers.

"The agent convinced me that Chicagoland had the money. The other firm didn't seem to have the money available… they said they had to go back to a couple of their investors to give them that amount. I love investors, but I didn't want to wait for them.

"When I heard that the agent had the money outside, I decided to go with them because I knew that they actually had the money already. That made a big difference.

"I made the right decision to sell my house with them instead of going with the other investor because he said, "Okay, let me call someone." I said, "That's okay. She said she has the money right now. I'll go with her."

"You can put your house on the market and wait to sell it. I just wanted to sell my house and be done with it. I really enjoyed the experience working with a professional agency. They treated me really well, and if I do want to sell another house, I would work with them again."

**HER LESSON:** Some cash investors operate independently while others can go through several rounds of investor approval before their offer is actually available to the seller. When talking to a cash investor, it's important to ask about the details of their process so you know whether an offer on their end is truly there to take. In Carolyn's case, their timeline did not fit hers, and she needed to find a cash investor who could accommodate her situation.

# 7

## RAY: THE IMPORTANCE OF PROFESSIONALISM

After Ray's mother-in-law passed, he and his wife had to figure out how to sell her three-bedroom, one-bathroom house. They were busy with a litany of other pressing issues, so they couldn't waste any time… but they weren't going to unload the house to the very first buyer, either. They wanted to make sure that they got a fair price, worked with professional investors, and sold to a company that would maintain the integrity of the neighborhood.

**IN HIS WORDS:** "We inherited my mother-in-law's house. She passed away and my wife was in control of the process, so we had to sell it. I didn't want to put it on the open market… it was a nice house, but we had to hurry up and sell it because we had so many other things going on. So, we decided to find somebody to sell to.

"We talked to several people. We found a couple who were really nice, and then we went with the best of them all. It seemed like a good outfit and they were close by, which helped make it a very good experience for us.

"We were going to go the traditional way, and I said, "Well, let's see how fair these people are." Of course, it's people who have signs up on every block that say they'll buy your house for cash. But they're not willing to give you what I think is a fair price. Some even had a cocky attitude.

"This was a new experience for me, and I know that some of them want to try to buy everything for nothing, but I don't think that's right. I was willing to sell at a fair price of someone was willing to give me a fair price. My mother-in law had nice neighbors... we didn't want to mess with that, so we wanted to make sure that we sold to someone who would fix the house up nicely and sell it to some good people – not just to somebody who wanted to come in and grab some property.

"You even see these conventions now where people teach how to flip houses and how to make some money quickly... I could see their point, but I still think you should get a fair price for what you have. Another investor was close on the bidding and she said, "If you get any other bids, let me know. Maybe I can match it." And I asked her, "What's the best you can do?" She didn't come up to what we were looking for, so I told her that if she couldn't do that number, we didn't have a deal. She said, "I don't think anybody else is going to do that," but they did.

"I didn't know what I needed when it came to lawyers, but the investor's team said they had lawyers who weren't working for them, but who would work with their customers. They took care of everything – they explained how everything went and it went along with no hitches. They got a clear title on the house and said there was nothing to worry about. We didn't even have to be at the closing, but we were.

"We did get a surprise on taxes. My mother-in-law was getting all kinds of senior freezes and homeowners discounts that didn't apply to us. We were charged regular taxes, which we weren't expecting, and that made a big difference.

"We could have waited a little longer, but the tax bill came... if we would have waited and paid the tax bill, we might have done a little better. Maybe next time we'll know better, but it's hard when it's your first time doing something like this.

"The main thing is to make sure that you're dealing with somebody reputable and that you like. And it's good when the closing is close to you. If we would've worked with something who wasn't very good, or who was with a shabby outfit, then we probably would have hated this type of experience. "It can go either way, but it's better to be honest up front and do it right."

**HIS LESSON:** Ray's story shows how important it is to make sure that an offer is fair. Every seller needs to understand that buyers are in it for the investment opportunity – they've got to make money on the deal, too – but that doesn't mean every offer is a good one. By talking to several investors, Ray and his wife were able to get an offer they were comfortable with while still selling the property quickly.

# 8

## SUSAN: CAN YOUR INVESTOR HELP YOU HANDLE SURPRISES?

S usan and her husband wanted to move to Florida, but they needed to sell their house first. When they started that process, they encountered a surprise related to a refinanced loan... and that affected their ability to sell their old house and buy a new one.

**IN HER WORDS:** "We purchased our house almost 30 years ago, but we needed to move out of state to get to a warmer climate. It was our home, so we held onto it until the end because you just don't know how quickly something will go and we didn't want to be without a place to stay.

"We waited until the last minute to sell, but the house was a little over a hundred years old. It had some stuff that needed to be repaired, and we thought, "You know what? Let's just go with something we know is going to be a sure thing and get rid of it." We'd have had to worry about bringing stuff up to code and all that, and it was just a hassle we didn't need.

"It's super expensive to repair anything in a house like that, even the windows. Nothing was a normal fix because they weren't the normal sizes. Putting on storm doors? They didn't measure the same.

"I started to Google and made a phone call, and I connected with the agent from the first minute we talked. She was so nice and accommodating by asking, "What works for you?" That made it wonderful to work with her. We didn't even look at other companies because she and I connected immediately. It felt right, and I felt like she was being straight-up honest. I didn't feel like she was trying to play games.

"The process ended up dragging on because when we went to sell, we did not realize that there was a lien on our home. We had paid off our home four or five years ago. We had an old loan that we'd been paying without making much progress, and the woman at the bank said that they could give us better terms. I signed the papers without reading the fine print because we'd worked with her so much. Unbeknownst to me, it was either a second mortgage or a straight-up mortgage… I don't even know.

"When we went to sell, they gave us the price and we thought everything was a done deal. We were going to take that money and pay the loan that we owed. The next thing we know, there's a lien on the house. I said, "There can't be a lien on it. We've paid for our house." That's how dumbfounded I was. But we went back and forth, and sure enough, that's what it was.

"The agent just kept saying, "Sue, just relax. This is going to work out. Let me see what I can do on my end, let me see if I can find out anything." She bent over backwards to help me. It was unreal. Unreal. Honest to God, I told her that when she was done helping us, she needed a vacation. I told her to come stay with us in Florida because that's how good I felt with her, believe it or not. To think that I'd just say, "Oh, you can come into my home and I have no problem!"

"Then we ran into some problems because that home that we purchased in Florida is a manufactured home, so many banks wouldn't work with us. In fact, I had been with the same bank for probably 30 years, and they had one down here. I thought I'd talk to them because surely, they would be familiar with me... they no longer dealt with manufactured homes, either. I ended up with another bank that, luckily, I felt good with. It's 98 years old, family-owned, and not a fly-by-night.

"We were able to get everything squared away. Needless to say, the agent just never gave up on us. I would touch base every couple weeks to see if someone was coming out for an appraisal or if something needed to be done. She told me that her team had meetings on Tuesdays, so I was able to touch base with her by Monday to let her know what was going on. She seemed just as appreciative to be able to have open contact like that. I thought I was going to have to move back, but she just never gave up. Without her coaching me and explaining things the way she had? I don't know. We wouldn't have been here in Florida, I guarantee we would've been back.

"When it came to getting a loan, she knew of a friend of hers in banking who gave me suggestions. She even had her license in Florida, so she offered to help me if we needed it. The pieces just fell right where they needed to be. It was stuff like, "If they can't help you, let me see if she can," and, "If there's anything more I can do for you, let me know." They weren't telling me what they needed. They were asking what they could do to make it easier for me.

"My advice is for sellers to understand their own property, to understand what they have in it, and whether there are things like outstanding liens. Then you can make a decision about whether to sell to an investor or go the traditional real estate route. We needed someone who was going to be more of an investor. Our check was smaller than I'd hoped for, but my Husband felt it was pretty darn close – and we avoided a lot of headaches.

"She kept telling us, "Thank you for not giving up." If it weren't for her, we would have."

**HER LESSON:** Susan stressed how important is to read the fine print and to know exactly what situation you're in as a homeowner and a seller. She was fortunate to have an agent on her side to advocate for her and guide her through what turned out to be a much more complex process than she thought it would be. Everything turned out extremely well for her, but it could've gone sour just as easily.

Her relationship with the agent and the investment company turned what could have been an impossible process into just another normal problem to solve. She chose to work with the team because of that comfort and trust – something that isn't always present in buyer/seller relationships – and it made all the difference.

# NOW THAT YOU'RE READY TO SELL TO A CASH INVESTOR...

These testimonials detail a range of different scenarios. Some surely match up with yours, while others have unique elements that don't quite fit. Despite this diversity in circumstances and outcomes, we can pull five important bits of wisdom from their stories that apply to all home sales, including yours:

**Do Your Homework.** A common thread in many of these stories is how critical it is to be educated. You won't go from novice to real estate expert in a few hours of searching the internet, but you can get a solid sense of the basics. From researching your options to vetting potential investors by reading other clients' testimonials, you can put yourself in a much stronger position during the home-selling process and feel better about the result by exercising due diligence.

**Be Honest with Yourself.** The more open and honest you are with yourself about the situation you're in with a property, the easier it will be to find the best solution. Are you able to manage renovations? Can you afford to put the necessary money into the property? How long can you leave the home on the market, and what will you do if you don't sell it quickly? You need to ask these and several other questions to help determine whether a traditional sale works or selling to an investor is a better fit.

**Explore Your Options.** Susan hit the jackpot by connecting with the first agent she spoke with. Cindy, on the other hand, encountered an insulting offer from the first investor she contacted. Most of the other stories are somewhere in between, with the best result usually coming after talking with a few different investors. By talking to more than one investor, you can find the best offer for your home and identify the right fit for you.

**Work with a Professional.** The sellers who are happiest with their experience overwhelmingly echo the same sentiment: they felt much better working with agents and investors who they felt were professionals. Working with a competent, reputable investor and team means less worry and a smoother process. There's usually a reason why professional outfits achieve that level of success and the ones who don't seem to be professionals… well, don't.

**Feel Comfortable.** No matter what route you choose to sell your home, the most important element is that you feel as comfortable as possible about the process and the result. These eight stories varied in degrees of comfort – Denise was in a very difficult situation, while Diane just wanted to sell the property. They and the other six were all happy with the outcome precisely because they felt comfortable along the way, and they've continued to feel comfortable with their decision to sell.

Selling a home can be difficult, but it doesn't have to be if you follow a few simple rules. Ask questions. Do research and identify professionals. Find agents and investors who you trust and who make you feel comfortable. If you learn from these testimonials and apply their hard-earned lessons, your success story of selling to a cash investor will fit right in.

# ABOUT SAUL Z

Saul Zenkevicius is an investor, investment real estate broker, and real estate entrepreneur. For 15 years he has successfully navigated various niches within real estate investing and has participated in more than 2,500 real estate transactions. Saul started his career as a real estate appraiser and swiftly transitioned into investing, eventually founding multiple companies in the real estate space.

He has brokered real estate dispositions for Fannie Mae, Freddie Mac, Bank of America, Chase, and many other institutional investors. Currently, Saul is a managing partner of Z Equity Group, which is growing rapidly in the Commercial Real Estate space.

Saul is also a partner in Chicagoland Home Buyer, Atlas Title & Escrow, Universal Mortgage Partners, and Z Team Realty. Lastly, Saul is co-founder of real estate CRM Firepoint, which is a nationwide leader in the customer relationship management space
In 2013, Saul was running the traditional Z Team as a real estate broker when his team was ranked #34 in the country by Wall Street Journal with 476 transactions in the previous year. As CEO of

Chicagoland Home Buyer, Saul buys and renovates homes in Chicagoland and other markets nationwide. He is passionate about both his business and real estate; his satisfaction comes from helping other people solve their problems and transforming homes into properties that new buyers can fall in love with. Saul is a husband to Rosi and a father of three beautiful kids, Marty, Nikolas and Victoria. When he's not working, Saul spends time with his kids in a range of outdoor activities. Saul competes in 1-2 Iron Man races each year, and he also enjoys kiteboarding and traveling with his family.

Made in the USA
Middletown, DE
03 September 2019